Bungalo
Books

*Dedicated to the primary teachers who give children
their first gentle push toward independent reading.*

Written by Frank B. Edwards
Illustrated by John Bianchi
©1997 by Bungalo Books

Cataloguing in Publication Data

Edwards, Frank B.
   Peek-a-boo at the Zoo

(Bungalo Books new reader series)
ISBN 0-921285-53-1 (bound)   ISBN 0-921285-52-3 (pbk.)

I. Bianchi, John   II.Title.   III.Series

PS8559.D84P43 1997   jC813'.54   C97-900438-1
PZ7.E253Pe 1997

Published in Canada by:
Bungalo Books
Ste.100
17 Elk Court
Kingston, Ontario
K7M 7A4

Co-published in U.S.A. by:
Firefly Books (U.S.) Inc.
Ellicott Station
P.O. Box 1338
Buffalo, New York
14205

Peek-a-boo
at the Zoo

Written by Frank B. Edwards
Illustrated by John Bianchi

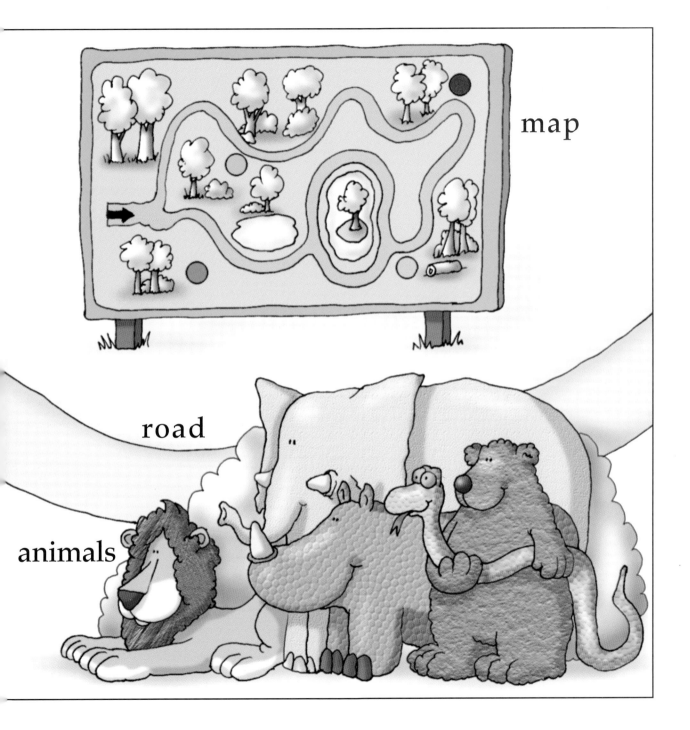

map

road

animals

Peek-a-boo. Where are you?

Monkey

Look again. I am here

Peek-a-boo. Where are you?

Lion
Tiger

Peek-a-boo. Where are you?

Look again. We are here.

Peek-a-boo. Where are you?

Look again. We are here.

Now where did you all go?

Look around.
We are all in here!

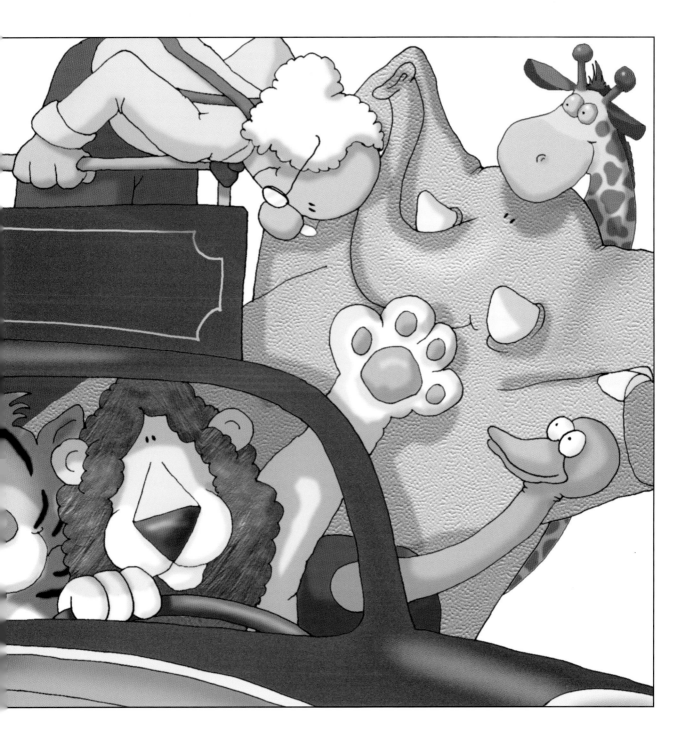

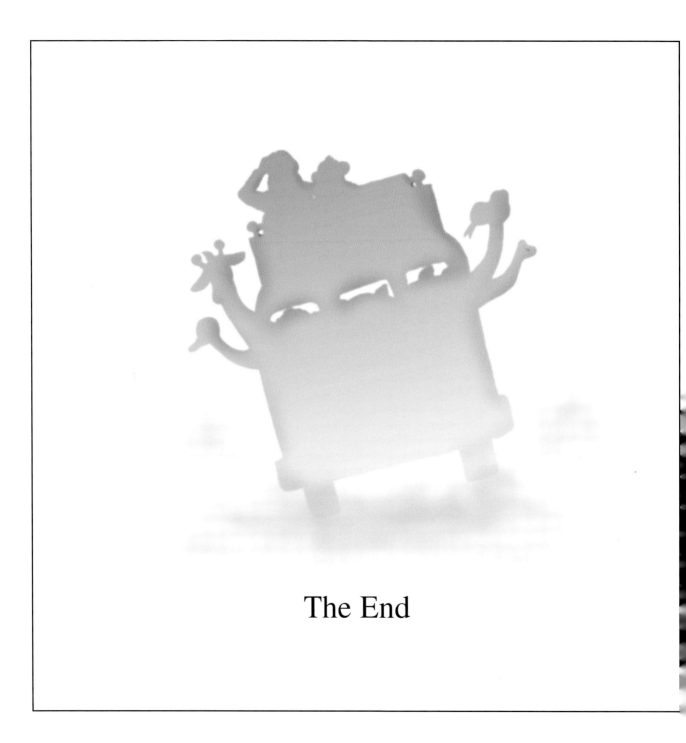

The End

The Author and Illustrator

Frank B. Edwards is a former writer and editor with Harrowsmith and Equinox magazines. John Bianchi is a cartoonist who works from his studio in Arizona's Sonoran Desert.

In 1986, they co-founded Bungalo Books and eventually gave up serious employment to create children's books on a full-time basis. They now have twenty-five books to their credit.

John and Frank can be reached on the Internet at: bungalo@cgocable.net

Official Bungalo Reading Buddies

Kids who love to read books are eligible to become official, card-carrying Bungalo Reading Buddies. If you and your friends want to join an international club dedicated to having fun while reading, show this notice to your teacher or librarian. We'll send your class a great membership kit.

Teachers and Librarians

Bungalo Books would be pleased to send you a Reading Buddy membership kit that includes 30 full-colour, laminated membership cards. These pocket-sized, 2¼-by-4-inch membership cards can be incorporated into a wide variety of school and community reading programmes for primary, junior and intermediate elementary school students.

* **Each kit includes 30 membership cards, postcards, bookmarks, a current Bungalo Reading Buddy newsletter and a Bungalo storybook.**
* **Kits cost only $7.50 for postage and handling.**
* **No cash please. Make cheque or money order payable to Bungalo Books.**
* **Offer limited to libraries and schools.**
* **Please allow four weeks for delivery.**

Bungalo World Headquarters
17 Elk Court
Suite 100
Kingston, Ontario
K7M 7A4